TRAUMA
Therapy Workbook

_____
_____
_____

All rights are reserved 2024 by Life Style Daily. No part of this publication may be reproduced, stored in a retrieval system or transmitted in any form or by any means, electronic, mechanical, photocopying, recording or otherwise, without prior permission.

PTSD & Trauma Processing Worksheets Workbook

This workbook is designed as a supportive and practical tool for adults navigating the complex and often overwhelming journey of trauma recovery and PTSD management. By combining therapeutic exercises with reflective prompts, this guide empowers individuals to process their emotions, understand their triggers, and develop personalized safety plans tailored to their unique needs. The structured worksheets encourage self-exploration and provide actionable steps to build resilience, foster emotional regulation, and strengthen self-acceptance. With a focus on creating a safe and nurturing space, the workbook also offers strategies for coping with distress, identifying supportive resources, and cultivating a sense of empowerment and healing. Whether you are working independently or in collaboration with a therapist, this workbook aims to be a trusted companion in your journey toward recovery, self-awareness, and emotional well-being.

All rights are reserved 2024 by Life Style Daily. No part of this publication may be reproduced, stored in a retrieval system or transmitted in any form or by any means, electronic, mechanical, photocopying, recording or otherwise, without prior permission.

DAILY PLANNER

Date:

Today's Goals

Today's Appointment

Water Intake

Fruit/ Vegetable

Mood

Today I Am Grateful For

Things To Get Done Today

WEEKLY PLANNER

Weekly Priorities
-
-
-
-
-
-

Notes

Monday | Tuesday | Wednesday | Thursday | Friday | Saturday | Sunday

Checklist
-
-
-
-
-
-
-
-

Appointment

Reminder

MONTHLY PLANNER

MONTH:

Mon	Tue	Wed	Thu	Fri	Sat	Sun

Notes

_____

_____

_____

MY TRAUMAS

USE THE SPACE BELOW TO DESCRIBE YOUR TRAUMAS. THE FIRST STEP TOWARDS HEALING IS TO ACKNOWLEDGE YOUR TRAUMAS.

MY TRAUMAS

TAKE THE TIME TO ACKNOWLEDGE WHAT HAD HAPPENED, HOW IT MADE YOU FEEL IN THE PAST AND HOW IT MAKES YOU FEEL NOW.

EVENTS THAT HAD HAPPENED	HOW DID IT MAKE ME FEEL?	HOW AM I FEELING NOW?

MY TRAUMAS

USE THE SPACE BELOW TO DESCRIBE YOUR TRAUMAS. THE FIRST STEP TOWARDS HEALING IS TO ACKNOWLEDGE YOUR TRAUMAS.

TRAUMA WORKSHEET

| What Am I Traumatized About? | What Can I Do To Overcome It? |

My Action Plan

A Promise To My Self

WORKING ON YOUR TRIGGERS

| WHAT'D HAPPENED RECENTLY? | WHAT'D HAPPENED IN THE PAST? |

HOW DID I FEEL WHEN THE EVENT FIRST HAPPENED IN THE PAST?

| HOW AM I FEELING NOW JOURNALING ABOUT IT? | WHAT I NEEDED IN THE MOMENT THAT I DIDN'T GET OR DO? |

WHAT SELF CARE ACTIVITIES CAN I ENGAGE IN TO SELF SOOTHE?
Examples: try a meditation class, take a relaxing hot bath, get a mani/pedicure, etc.

TRIGGER PROCESSING

DESCRIBE WHAT'D HAPPENED

WHAT MENTAL, VERBAL OR PHYSICAL RESPONSE OCCURRED?

WHY DID YOU RESPOND THE WAY YOU DID?

WHAT EMOTIONS DID YOU FEEL?

BREAK DOWN THE COMMENT, ACT, OR EXPERIENCE THAT TRIGGERED YOU

WORKING ON PATTERNS

WHAT PATTERNS DO YOU SEE REPEATING THEMSELVES IN YOUR LIFE?

_____
_____
_____
_____
_____
_____
_____

HOW HAD THESE PATTERNS AFFECTED YOU AND/OR PEOPLE AROUND YOU?	WHICH PATTERNS DID YOU PICK UP FROM YOUR CAREGIVERS?

WHAT ACTIONS CAN YOU TAKE TO BREAK THESE PATTERNS?

_____
_____
_____
_____
_____
_____
_____
_____

LEARN TO RESPOND NOT REACT

REACTIONS TEND TO GO LIKE THIS: AN EVENT HAPPENS. YOU PANIC. THEN YOU PROCEED. RESPONSES TEND TO GO LIKE THIS: AN EVENT HAPPENS. YOU PAUSE. YOU PROCESS. YOU PLAN. THEN YOU PROCEED.

STEP 1: BECOME AWARE THAT YOUR THOUGHTS ARE NOT YOU	Observe your thoughts in the moment. Take a step back to create a mental space between you and your thoughts. Acknowledge all the thoughts that surface up but become aware that your thoughts are not you.
STEP 2: COME BACK TO YOUR BODY & THE PRESENT MOMENT	When facing a trigger that makes you more reactive than usual, choose to pause & take a few deep breaths. Bring your attention back to your body and the present moment.
STEP 3: REAFFIRM TO YOURSELF "I LOVE YOU" & "YOU'RE SAFE"	Place your right palm over your chest at the heart center and tell yourself "I love you" & "you're safe" to soothe and comfort yourself. Once you've successfully self-soothed yourself, then plan on how you can best handle the situation.

I'M AWARE THAT MY THOUGHTS ARE NOT ME

WRITE DOWN WHAT MAKES YOU FEEL WORRIED, SAD, SCARED, DEPRESSED, ANGRY, AND/OR ANXIOUS

Use the questions below to examine and break down the thought. Ask yourself:

Is my thought based on a feeling or an actual fact?

Is it possible for my thought to come true?

What's the worst that can happen if it does come true?

Will it still matter to me tomorrow or in the future?

What can I do to handle the situation in a positive way?

HEAL YOUR INNER CHILD IN 7 STEPS

STEP 1: ACKNOWLEDGE YOUR INNER CHILD

Giving your inner child a real identity can help you work through the issues you faced together. Start by speaking statements of affirmation such as " I love you" " I see you" and "I feel your pains" in the mirror, or visualize hugging & saying this to your younger, wondered self.

_____
_____
_____
_____
_____
_____
_____
_____
_____
_____
_____
_____
_____
_____
_____
_____
_____
_____
_____

HEAL YOUR INNER CHILD IN 7 STEPS

STEP 2: VALIDATE WHAT HAPPENED

Pushing the issues away can only work for so long. It is time to face what had happened. With your inner child by your side, take the time to recognize and acknowledge what had happened. Write down the traumatic events along with the way they made you feel and what impacts the events had on you.

WHAT'D HAPPENED?	HOW DID I FEEL WHEN IT HAPPENED?	WHAT IMPACTS THE EVENT HAD ON MY LIFE?

HEAL YOUR INNER CHILD IN 7 STEPS

STEP 3: IDENTIFY THE TYPE OF NEGLECT YOU EXPERIENCED

Take the time to identify the type of neglect you felt growing up, whether it was a lack of love, a lack of care, a lack of compassion or a lack of parental protection. Allow yourself to feel into that void and recognize it for what it is.

HEAL YOUR INNER CHILD IN 7 STEPS

STEP 4: EMBRACE YOUR EMOTIONS

While you're working on healing your inner child, many different types of emotions may surface up. Allow yourself to sit with them, acknowledge and feel into them rather than running away from them.

Things/Events/People That Make Me Feel Sad	Things/Events/People That Make Me Feel Angry

Things/Events/People That Make Me Feel Anxious	Things/Events/People That Make Me Feel Scared

HEAL YOUR INNER CHILD IN 7 STEPS

STEP 5: IDENTIFY CURRENT MANIFESTATIONS OF PAST HURTS

Take the time to identify the areas of your life where you may have engaged in self sabotaged behaviors because of your past childhood hurts and wounds. It's important for you to be honest with yourself. Acknowledgement is the first step toward moving forward and making the shift toward healthier habits.

Love	Career

Finance	Family

Health	Friendship

HEAL YOUR INNER CHILD IN 7 STEPS

STEP 6: TAKE STEPS TO FILL THE GAP

When you were younger, you didn't have the means and power to give yourself what you needed such as love, care, money, protection, quality time. However, now as an adult, you can take the time to identify what it is that you need and give to yourself. Identify what can fill your cup of happiness and fulfillment

Love	Career

Finance	Family

Health	Friendship

HEAL YOUR INNER CHILD IN 7 STEPS

STEP 7: MAKE PEACE WITH THE PAST BY HELPING OTHERS

You cannot go back to the past to change what happened to you. However, there are ways you can help change the present and the future of someone who is now suffering what you had gone through. Use the space below to brainstorm the steps you can take to give a lending hand to someone in need.

WORKING TOWARDS HEALING

WHAT TRAUMA DO I NEED TO HEAL FROM?

STEPS THAT I NEED TO TAKE TO HEAL

THINGS I HAVE HEALED FROM & HOW?

EXPERIENCE BREAKDOWN

WHAT HAPPENED TODAY?

WHAT I FELT ABOUT IT

I GOT TRIGGERED BECAUSE..

_____
_____
_____

THE ENVIRONMENT I WAS IN

THE PEOPLE I WAS WITH

MY THOUGHTS AND REFLECTION

_____
_____
_____

ACKNOWLEDGE YOUR THOUGHTS & FEELINGS

MY THOUGHTS

_____
_____
_____
_____
_____
_____
_____
_____

I'm feeling SAD
0   10

I'm feeling ANXIOUS
0   10

I'm feeling SCARED
0   10

I'm feeling ANGRY
0   10

I'm feeling FRUSTRATED
0   10

HOW AM I FEELING TODAY?

_____
_____
_____
_____
_____
_____
_____
_____
_____
_____

FACILITATING HEALING

WHAT HAPPENED IN THE PAST THAT IS STILL CAUSING ME SO MUCH PAIN?

_____
_____
_____
_____
_____
_____
_____

WHAT TRAUMA AM I WORKING ON HEALING FROM?

WHAT THINGS HAVE I HEALED FROM ALREADY? HOW?

MY ACTION PLAN TO FACILITATE HEALING

MEDICATION TRACKER

DATE	TIME	MEDICATION	DOSE	NOTES

MEDICATION HISTORY

MEDICATION	START DATE	START DOSE	NOTES

DOCTOR VISITS

VISITS DESCRIPTION	DATE	TIME	NOTES

DOCTORS NOTES

Reason For Appointment	Time	Notes

Points Discussed

Notes

_____
_____
_____
_____
_____
_____
_____

THERAPY PROGRESS NOTES

Therapist	Session Goal	Session Number

Points Discussed

Progress Notes

To Do/Work On

Other Notes

THERAPY APPOINTMENTS

Visits Description	Date	Time	Notes

THERAPY GOALS

Goal	Date	Time	Notes

PRE-THERAPY PREP

Date:_____

Pre-Therapy Appointments Notes

Question of my Therapist	Reoccurring triggering events, emotions, negative self talk that needs processing

SELF BLAME

WHAT ARE THE SELF BLAME THOUGHTS THAT FREQUENTLY OCCUR IN YOUR HEAD?

DO YOU FEEL RESPONSIBLE FOR YOUR TRAUMA? HOW SO?

DO YOU FEEL LIKE WHAT'S HAPPENED TO YOU COULD BE AVOIDED/PREVENTED? HOW SO?

DO YOU FEEL LIKE NOBODY TRULY UNDERSTANDS HOW YOU FEEL? EXPLAIN:

DO YOU ALWAYS FEEL LIKE YOU SHOULD HAVE/COULD HAVE DONE SOMETHING TO STOP WHAT'D HAPPENED? EXPLAIN:

DO YOU FEEL LIKE YOU COULD NEVER TRUST ANYONE AGAIN? EXPLAIN?

DO YOU QUESTION WHY THIS HAD HAPPENED TO YOU? HOW SO?

DO YOU AVOID TALKING ABOUT IT? EXPLAIN:

DO YOU AVOID SEEKING HELP WHEN NEEDED? EXPLAIN:

DO YOU FEEL LIKE YOU DESERVED IT? EXPLAIN:

SELF ACCEPTANCE

| WHAT ARE YOUR STRENGTHS? | WHAT ARE YOUR WEAKNESSES? |

| WHAT MAKES YOU UNIQUE & SPECIAL? | WHAT ARE THE IMPERFECTIONS THAT MAKE YOU UNIQUE? |

| WHAT CHARACTERISTICS, QUALITIES, TALENTS, SKILLS AND ABILITIES DO YOU POSSES THAT YOU ADMIRE IN YOURSELF? |

Self Compassion

| WHAT DO YOU OFTEN CRITICIZE YOURSELF ABOUT? | WHAT DO YOU FEEL MOST ASHAMED ABOUT YOURSELF? |

| WHAT EMOTIONS ARE YOU FEELING WHILE CRITICIZING YOURSELF? |

| WHAT TONE, PHRASES AND WORDS ARE YOU USING? | IF YOU WERE TO CONFRONT YOUR INNER CRITIC, WHAT WOULD YOU SAY? |

PROCESSING NIGHTMARES

What type of recurring nightmares do you usually have? what are they about?

_____
_____
_____
_____
_____
_____
_____

HOW IS HAVING NIGHTMARES AFFECTING YOUR SLEEP AT NIGHT?

HOW DO YOU FEEL THE NEXT MORNING AFTER HAVING A NIGHTMARE THE NIGHT BEFORE?

WHAT ARE YOUR NIGHTMARES TELLING YOU?

What underlying trauma is associated with your nightmares?

_____
_____
_____
_____
_____
_____
_____

SELF WORTH

| SELF WORTH POSITIVE AFFIRMATION |

| WHAT HARSH CRITICISM DO YOU OFTEN TELL YOURSELF WHILE PERFORMING TASKS/CHORES? | WHY DO YOU THINK YOU ARE OFTEN HARSH ON YOURSELF? |

| WHAT ARE YOUR GREATEST STRENGTHS? WHAT DO YOU MOST ADMIRE ABOUT YOURSELF? |

TRIGGER COPING CARDS

| TAKE DEEP BREATHS | BECOME AWARE OF YOUR TRIGGERS |

| PLAN A COPING STRATEGY FOR YOUR TRIGGERS | PRACTICE REGULAR MEDITATION |

| KEEP A JOURNAL | SHARE YOUR FEELINGS WITH A FRIEND/PARTNER/THERAPIST |

COPING WITH GRIEF AND LOSS

| WHAT TYPE OF LOSS ARE YOU TRYING TO HEAL FROM? | HOW DO YOU FEEL ABOUT WHAT HAPPENED? |

WHAT WORDS, EVENTS, ITEMS, PEOPLE CAN TRIGGER YOUR FEELING OF GRIEF AND LOSS? HOW SO?

DAILY REFLECTION

Date:_____

5 THINGS THAT MADE ME FEEL HAPPY TODAY

5 SMALL SUCCESSES I HAD TODAY WERE

TODAY I HAD FUN WHEN

TRIGGER PROCESSING

WHEN TRIGGERED, WHERE ARE YOU HOLDINGS STRESS AND TENSION?

PHYSICAL SYMPTOMS MANIFESTED BECAUSE OF MY EMOTIONAL STRESS

_____
_____
_____
_____
_____
_____
_____

WEEKLY SELF CARE

Week Of:_____

MON	
TUE	
WED	
THU	
FRI	
SAT	
SUN	

ANGER MANAGEMENT

DETERMINE WHETHER YOUR ANGER STEMS FROM PAST TRAUMA, UNRESOLVED EMOTIONAL ISSUES, MENTAL ILLNESS, OR AN UNHEALTHY SITUATION THAT NEEDS CHANGING

WHEN YOUR TEMPER BEGINS TO FLARE, MENTALLY CHALLENGE YOURSELF BEFORE BY ASKING THESE QUESTIONS

WHAT IS THE SOURCE OF MY IRRITATION?

WHAT IS THE DEGREE OF MY ANGER?

WHAT IS THE OTHER PERSON'S ACTUAL ROLE IN THIS SITUATION?

OVERCOMING FEAR

HOW IS THIS HOLDING YOU BACK IN LIFE?

WHAT IS YOUR GREATEST FEAR?

HOW WAS THIS FEAR DEVELOPED?

LIST OLD FEARS YOU ARE READY TO PUT BEHIND

SELF LOVE

SELF LOVE POSITIVE AFFIRMATION

_____
_____
_____
_____
_____
_____
_____

| WHAT DO YOU HATE SO MUCH ABOUT YOURSELF? WHAT IS THE REASON BEHIND THE HATRED? | CAN THAT FEELING BE CHANGED? HOW? |

WRITE A LETTER TO YOURSELF TO EXPRESS THE UNCONDITIONAL LOVE YOU'VE IN STORE FOR YOURSELF

ANXIETY TRACKER

Date & Time	What Made Me Feel Anxious	Outcome Of The Situation	Anxiety Rating

ANGER TRACKER

Date & Time	What Made Me Feel Anxious	Outcome Of The Situation	Anger Rating

MOOD TRACKER

Date:

Time:

My Mood

Date:

Time:

My Mood

Date:

Time:

My Mood

MEDICATION TRACKER

Date	✓	Medication	Time

DECATASTROPHIZING WORKSHEET

WHAT "CATASTROPHE" IS BOTHERING YOU?

What is the likelihood of the catastrophe occurring?

In the past, has this ever happened before?

HOW FREQUENTLY DOES THIS OCCUR IN REAL LIFE?

How terrible would it be if your catastrophe really occurred?

What would the worst possible outcome look like?

IF THE WORST HAPPENS, WHAT WILL YOU DO?

Who or what could help you?

What could you do in advance to prepare?

What skills do you already have that can help you through it?

DISCOVER MY AUTHENTIC SELF

- I AM SPEAKING MY OPINIONS HONESTLY IN A HEALTHY WAY
- I ALLOW MYSELF TO BE VULNERABLE & OPEN HEARTED
- I AM LISTENING TO THE INNER VOICE GUIDING ME FORWARDS
- I AM FULLY PRESENT WHEN I WORK OR GO THROUGH LIFE EXPERIENCES
- I AM PURSUING MY PASSIONS
- I AM MAKING DECISIONS THAT ARE ALIGNED WITH MY PRINCIPLES, VALUES AND BELIEFS
- I SET MY BOUNDARIES AND I RESPECT THEM
- I WALK AWAY FROM TOXIC SITUATIONS & RELATIONSHIPS

PHYSICAL COPING SKILLS FOR ANGER MANAGEMENT

DO YOGA	PUSH WALL	BOUNCE BALL
PRESS DOWN ON MY SEAT	SQUEEZE A STRESS BALL	STRETCH MY BODY
PUNCH A PILLOW	PRESS MY PALMS TOGETHER	RIP PAPER INTO SMALL PIECES

WORRY COPING CARDS

Take Deep Breaths	Be in the Present Moment
Draw Your Worries	Go to Your Favorite Place
Journal Your Thoughts	Share Your Thoughts with a friend/Partner/Therapist

HEART BREATHING

USE THIS BREATHWORK TECHNIQUE TO HELP YOU COPE WITH TRIGGERS

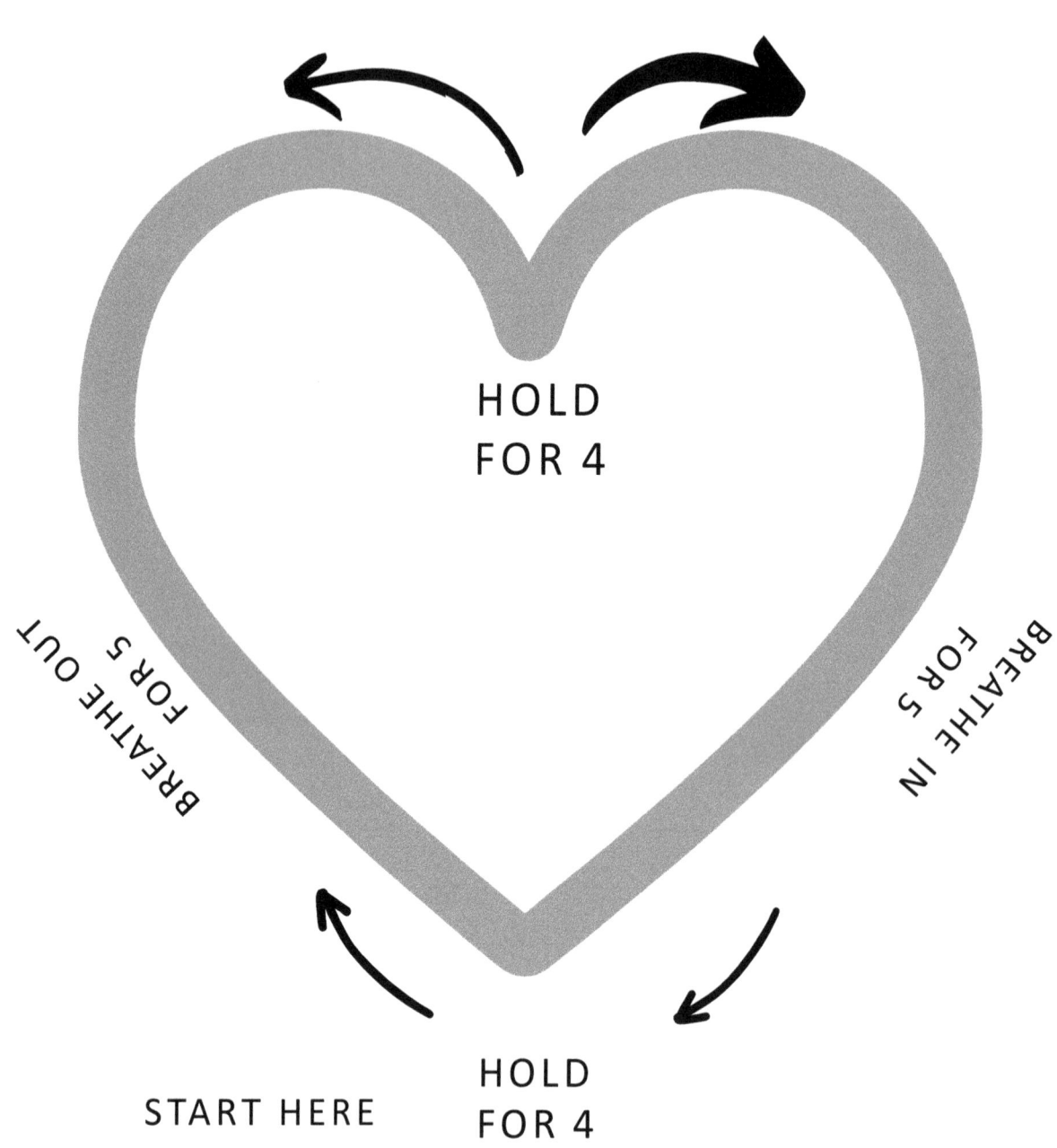

THINK OF SOMEONE OR SOMETHING YOU LOVE WHILE PRACTICING THIS BREATHING TECHNIQUE

THE BALLOON MENTAL EXERCISE

FOR WHEN YOU START TO FEEL WORRIED OR ANXIOUS

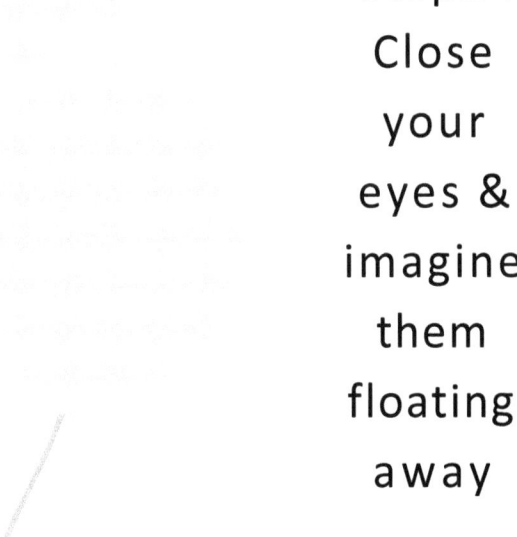

Step 1: Write down what worries you in the balloons

Step 2: Close your eyes & imagine them floating away

Step 3:

Come back to your breaths and repeat steps 1 and 2 as needed

BUILDING MY DREAM LIFE

REGARDLESS OF WHAT HAD HAPPENED, YOU DESERVE TO LIVE A
LIFE FULL OF LOVE, JOY, PEACH, HEALTH, ABUNDANCE AND HAPPINESS

MY NEW MORNING ROUTINE I AM COMMITTING TO

MY NEW EVENING ROUTINE I AM COMMITTING TO

WHAT IN MY CURRENT LIFE DO I WANT TO NOT TAKE INTO THE FUTURE WITH ME?

MY VISION BOARD

HEALTH	FAMILY	FINANCE

FRIENDSHIP	LOVE	CAREER

KNOWLEDGE	TRAVEL	HOBBIES

MONTHLY REFLECTIONS

HOW WAS THIS MONTH?

GRATEFUL FOR

AREAS OF IMPROVEMENT

CHALLENGES

MY FAVORITE MOMENT OF THIS MONTH

WHAT WENT WELL

HOW TO SET UP FOR SUCCESS NEXT MONTH

MONTHLY GOAL PLANNING

GOALS	REWARDS FOR ACHIEVING MY GOALS

WHY ACHIEVING THESE GOALS IMPORTANT TO ME?

WHAT STEPS DO I NEED TO TAKE TO ACCOMPLISH MY GOALS?

WEEKLY TASK PLANNING

TASKS THAT NEED TO GET DONE	TASK DEADLINES
_____	_____
_____	_____
_____	_____
_____	_____
_____	_____

STEPS THAT NEED TO BE TAKEN	REWARDS FOR COMPLETING THE TASKS
_____	_____
_____	_____
_____	_____
_____	_____
_____	_____
_____	_____
_____	_____

PLANS FOR NEXT WEEK

_____
_____
_____
_____
_____
_____

MY GOOD HABITS

GOOD HABITS TO MAINTAIN OR DEVELOP

BAD HABITS TO REDUCE OR ELIMINATE

ACTION PLAN TO MAINTAIN/DEVELOP MY GOOD HABITS

REWARDS FOR MAINTAINING MY GOOD HABITS

TO-DO LIST

Month of:_____

No	Date	To-Do	✓	✗

TO-DO LIST

Month of:_____

No	Date	To-Do	✓	✗

TO-DO LIST

Month of:_____

No	Date	To-Do	✓	✗

TO-DO LIST

Month of:_____

No	Date	To-Do	✓	✗

TO-DO LIST

Month of:_____

No	Date	To-Do	✓	✗

TO-DO LIST

Month of:_____

No	Date	To-Do	✓	✗

TO-DO LIST

Month of:_____

No	Date	To-Do	✓	✗

TO-DO LIST

Month of:_____

No	Date	To-Do	✓	✗

TO-DO LIST

Month of:_____

No	Date	To-Do	✓	✗

TO-DO LIST

Month of:_____

No	Date	To-Do	✓	✗

TO-DO LIST

Month of:_____

No	Date	To-Do	✓	✗

TO-DO LIST

Month of:_____

No	Date	To-Do	✓	✗

NOTES

NOTES

NOTES

NOTES

NOTES

NOTES

NOTES

NOTES

NOTES

NOTES

NOTES

NOTES

www.ingramcontent.com/pod-product-compliance
Ingram Content Group UK Ltd.
Pitfield, Milton Keynes, MK11 3LW, UK
UKHW050809210425
5547UKWH00034B/261